AMUSEMENT
Park

THIS EDITION
Editorial Management by Oriel Square
Produced for DK by WonderLab Group LLC
Jennifer Emmett, Erica Green, Kate Hale, *Founders*

Editors Grace Hill Smith, Libby Romero, Maya Myers, Michaela Weglinski;
Photography Editors Kelley Miller, Annette Kiesow, Nicole DiMella;
Managing Editor Rachel Houghton; **Designers** Project Design Company;
Researcher Michelle Harris; **Copy Editor** Lori Merritt; **Indexer** Connie Binder; **Proofreader** Larry Shea;
Reading Specialist Dr. Jennifer Albro; **Curriculum Specialist** Elaine Larson

Published in Great Britain by Dorling Kindersley Limited
DK, One Embassy Gardens, 8 Viaduct Gardens, London, SW11 7BW

The authorised representative in the EEA is
Dorling Kindersley Verlag GmbH. Arnulfstr. 124,
80636 Munich, Germany

A catalogue record for this book
is available from the British Library.
ISBN: 978-0-2416-0225-6

Printed and bound in China

The publisher would like to thank the following for their kind permission to reproduce their images:
a=above; c=centre; b=below; l=left; r=right; t=top; b/g=background

123RF.com: bevisphoto 20br; **Alamy Stock Photo:** agefotostock / Dennis MacDonald 9bl, imageBROKER / Heiner Heine
20-21, 31cla, Operation 2021 12bc; **Dreamstime.com:** Artmann-witte 3cb, Bigandt 10-11, Billyhoiler3 22-23, Ryhor Bruyeu
28-29, EMFielding 14-15, Felis 25bl, Greenland 17br, Kaleff 31cl, Andrew Kazmierski 10bc, Denys Kovtun 8-9, Libux77 1b,
Md_khairil X 29bl, Mirusiek 9br, Juriah Mosin 6-7, 31tl, David Murray 15bl, Alexander Oganezov 23bl, Pindiyath100 27bl,
Pressmaster 17bl, Radist 8bc, Radzian 22bc, Raycan 29br, Jorge Salcedo 25br, Sharifphoto 11br, Justin Skinner 28bc, 31bl,
Dariusz Szwangruber 26-27, Tammykayphoto 23br, Michael Turner 12-13, Ymgerman 18bc, Zuberka 11bl;
Getty Images: EyeEm / Justina Dzebrailove 30, EyeEm / Nattapol Poonpiriya 13br, Photo by cuellar 24-25,
Photodisc / Adam Gault 7br, The Image Bank / Steve Prezant 27br; **Getty Images / iStock:** E+ / AleksandarNakic 7bl,
E+ / andresr 24bc, E+ / baona 6br, E+ / kali9 26br, E+ / LawrenceSawyer 4bl, E+ / praetorianphoto 15br,
E+ / ProfessionalStudioImages 21b, E+ / SolStock 19br, henrycsmith 18-19, kali9 16-17, kuri2000 19bl,
Jennifer Peltier 13bl, 31clb; **Shutterstock.com:** FooTToo 4-5, Alexander Oganezov 16bc

Cover images: *Front:* **Dreamstime.com:** Microvone, Sabelskaya b; **Shutterstock.com:** Julia Soul Art;
Back: **Shutterstock.com:** maradaisy clb, NotionPic cra

All other images © Dorling Kindersley
For more information see: www.dkimages.com

For the curious
www.dk.com

AMUSEMENT
Park

Libby Romero

Come to the amusement park. See how forces and motion help people have fun!

There are many forces. Forces make things move.

forces

A push is a force.
A push makes
this girl move.

push

pull

A pull is a force.
A pull makes this
boy move down.

gravity

Gravity is a force. Gravity pulls things towards Earth.

smooth

Gravity pulls people
down slides.
A slide is
a smooth ride.

Gravity pulls a roller coaster down a hill. A roller coaster is very bumpy.

bumpy

Whee!

Forces can change how things move. Riders pull to make this ride start moving. They pull hard to make it move fast.

move

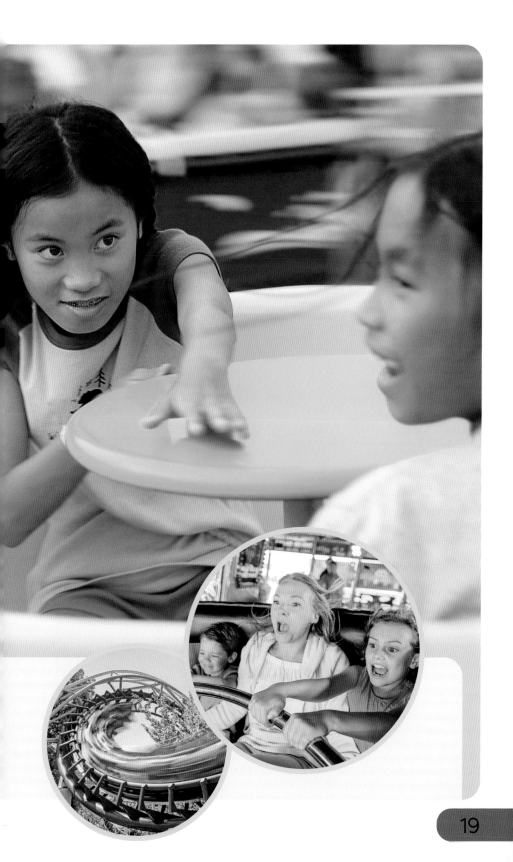

Crash!
The bumper
cars collide!
Forces make them
change directions.

collide

Screech!
The ride is stopped.
Forces make the
wheels stop moving.

stop

Strong forces push riders out from this ride's centre.

strong

Weak forces make things move, too.

weak

There are many forces in an amusement park. Forces put things in motion.

motion

Motion makes the day a lot of fun!

Glossary

force
a push or a pull

collide
to touch or come
together forcefully

centre
the point in the
middle of a circle

gravity
the force that pulls
things towards Earth

motion
movement

Quiz

Answer the questions to see what you have learnt. Check your answers with an adult.

1. True or False: A push is a force.

2. What do forces do?

3. Which force makes a roller coaster go down hills?

4. What makes bumper cars change directions?

5. Name three ways that forces and motion make amusement parks fun.

1. True 2. They make things move 3. Gravity 4. Forces
5. Answers will vary